D0810887

CORNWALL FROM THE AIR

Photographs by Bob Croxford
Barry Pearson ~ Pilot

A bird's eye view of the magnificent coastline of Cornwall shows many aspects. Harbours, cliffs and estuaries abound. Inland too there are ancient sites, castles and industrial developments which all have a unique interest. This small book travels in a clockwise direction around the coast from the River Tamar to Bude with a few inland sites included.

Many of the pictures in this, and other Atmosphere books, are available as large photo prints to frame. For details of sizes and prices please see www.atmosphere.co.uk/prints.html

Published by Atmosphere
Willis Vean
Mullion Cornwall TR12 7DF
England
Tel 01326 240180
email info@atmosphere.co.uk

ISBN 978 0 9543409 4 0

Printed and bound in Italy

Cover   St. Michael's Mount

Frontispiece   Aerial view of WEST PENWITH near Land's End

The Maze at GLENDURGAN Garden

These twin bridges across the TAMAR RIVER lead to Cornwall

LOOE showing the distinctive Banjo Pier and the beach at low tide

POLPERRO Harbour nestles in a narrow valley

FOWEY slopes down to the Fowey Estuary

The well protected harbour of MEVAGISSEY

The tiny cove and village of PORTLOE

Recently a working port CHARLESTOWN HARBOUR is now a base for tall ships

TRURO CATHEDRAL rises above the heart of Cornwall's County Town

The Fal Estuary stretches for miles inland

KING HARRY FERRY crosses the Fal Estuary

TRELISSICK HOUSE is set in stylish gardens

ST. MAWES CASTLE opposite the Fal Estuary from Pendennis Castle

PENDENNIS CASTLE was built by Henry VIII between 1540 and 1545

Custom House Quay at FALMOUTH

THE NATIONAL MARITIME MUSEUM in Falmouth

The village of HELFORD is a centre for sailing on the HELFORD ESTUARY

COVERACK is a small, characterful harbour on the Lizard Peninsula

The two beaches of CADGWITH separated by the Todden

The twin towers of THE LIZARD LIGHTHOUSE have warned ships away from this dangerous coast since 1751

KYNANCE COVE with Asparagus Island

MULLION COVE

LOE POOL, Cornwall's largest freshwater lake was formed when LOE BAR, a bank of shingle, blocked the sea's entrance

PORTHLEVEN HARBOUR

ST MICHAEL'S MOUNT

ST MICHAEL'S MOUNT with Marazion beyond

At the end of the railway line PENZANCE is a town of many facets

MOUSEHOLE nestles in a sheltered spot surrounded by sea and patchwork fields while Newlyn and then Penzance can be seen in the distance

More aspects of MOUSEHOLE

The clifftop Minack Theatre at PORTHCURNO

LAMORNA COVE lies at the end of a wooded valley

The dramatic cliffs near LAND'S END in West Pemwith drop into a crystal clear sea

The sweep of WHITSANDS BAY and Sennen Beach with St. Just in the distance

Cornwall's mining heritage at the ruins of THE GREAT FLAT LODE workings

CHYSAUSTER Iron Age Village with ruins of hut enclosures nearly 2,000 years old

ST. IVES from the air at low tide shows that the beach is never far away

The Island at ST. IVES with the town beyond

NEWQUAY has a string of beaches all along the coast including Tolcarne shown here

The Harbour at NEWQUAY

PORTH BEACH

The vast expanse of WATERGATE BAY

BEDRUTHAN STEPS showing the distinctive rock stacks

PARK HEAD in the distance beyond BEDRUTHAN STEPS

ROCK on the Camel Estuary

TINTAGEL HEAD is connected to the land by a narrow footbridge

BOSCASTLE suffered devastating flooding in 2004

BUDE showing the canal and river

The dramatic moonscape of CHINA CLAY mines near St Austell

Settlement tanks The Biomes at THE EDEN PROJECT are the biggest greenhouses in the world

RESTORMEL CASTLE dominates a valley just north of Lostwithiel

THE CHEESEWRING is a natural balancing stone formation near to ancient enclosures on Bodmin Moor

Cornwall's highest point is ROUGH TOR on Bodmin Moor

I have been taking pictures of Cornwall from the air for several years. I now have enough images to show them in this small book. The novelty of a bird's eye view of familiar places never ceases to amaze me. The relationship of sea to beach to cliffs is laid out, not like a map, but like a tapestry stretching away to the horizon.

On all these trips my pilot has been Barry Pearson whose skill and patience at getting me to the right place is unsurpassed. His ability to angle his small plane to avoid getting the wing intruding in my view amazes me. By day, and sometimes by night, he flies much bigger planes from Exeter Airport. In his spare time he operates a small airstrip and flying club at Eaglescott in North Devon.
His enthusiasm for flying is infectious.

THE HELFORD ESTUARY looking towards Falmouth Bay (overleaf)

INDEX